HOW IS MERCURY USED TODAY?

Chemistry Book for Kids 9-12 | Children's Chemistry Books

Speedy Publishing LLC

40 E. Main St. #1156

Newark, DE 19711

www.speedypublishing.com

Copyright 2017

Mercury is known as a transition metal and its symbol on the Periodic Table of Elements is Hg. Even though it is now considered to be poisonous, there remain many uses for it in today's world. Read further to learn more about this shiny, heavy, silvery liquid.

80
2
8
18
32
18
2
Hg
Mercury
200.59

THE BASICS

Its atomic number is 80 and its atomic weight is 200.59. When at room temperature it will become a liquid. The melting point of Mercury is -38.83°C, -37.89°F and its boiling point: 356.7°C, 674.1°F

On the period table, Mercury is the third element located in the twelfth column. Its atoms contain 80 protons and 80 electrons with 122 neutrons in its most abundant isotope.

E ven though it is the only metal that remains liquid when at room temperature, it has the smallest liquid range of any of the metals.

Swordfish, shark, and tuna are some of the species of fish that may contain a high level of mercury. While it doesn't mean that you don't want to eat these types of fish, this can become dangerous for a few people.

Tuna

Ruins of old facilities of mercury manufacturing

Norway, Denmark, and Sweden are some of the countries that have banned using mercury in manufacturing. The phrase "mad as a hatter" resulted from the hat makers

that became crazy from breathing its vapors that came from the chemicals used in making the hats.

CHARACTERISTICS AND PROPERTIES

Under typical conditions it appears as a heavy, shiny, silvery liquid. Mercury is the one metal that remains liquid when at room temperature, and evaporates into the air.

I t is highly poisonous and humans can absorb it through their skin, through the air, or by ingesting food containing mercury. Too much of this metal can be lethal to a human.

As it comes in contact with some of the other metals, mercury will dissolve them and create a different substance which is known as an amalgam. It is typically stored in an iron container since iron is one of the few exceptions and does not react to it.

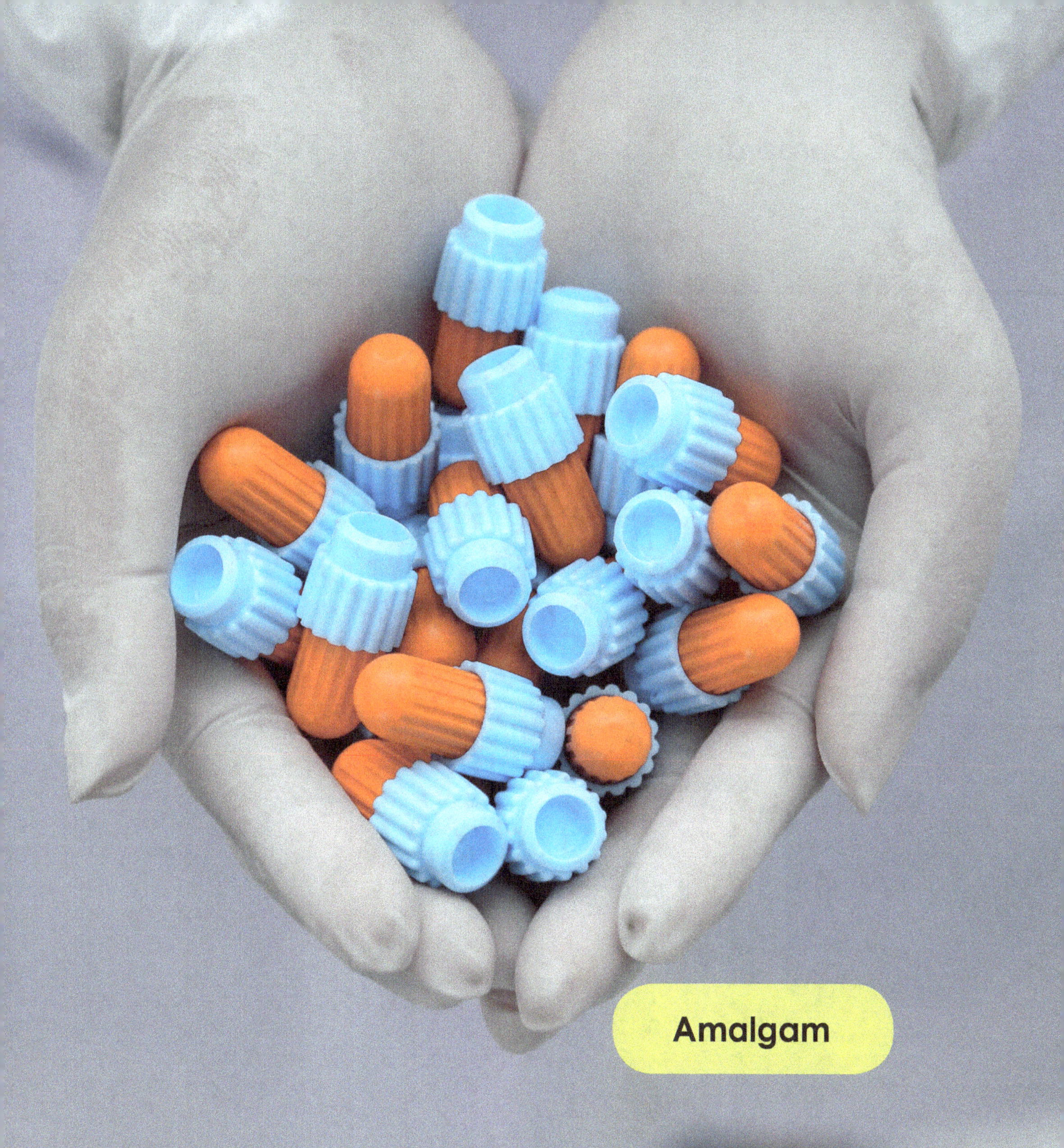
Amalgam

Corderoite

WHERE CAN IT BE FOUND?

Mercury is rare and can be found in the Earth's crust. Occasionally, it can be found in its free state, however, it is typically found in ores like corderoite, livingstonite, and cinnabar. Today, most of it is produced from mining of a bright red ore, cinnabar.

The greatest producers of mercury for several years were Spain and Italy. Spain mined it for use in the mining process of silver in South America. Most of the mercury mined today is in Kyrgyzstan and China.

HOW DO WE USE IT TODAY?

Mercury is used in a variety of applications, but is being slowly phased out of some because of health concerns. Because of its thermal expansion characteristics, and its high density, it is still used for measuring instruments including barometers and thermometers.

One of the biggest uses in today's world is mercury vapor lamps and fluorescent lamps. Some additional uses include vaccines, cosmetics, telescopes, and dental fillings.

HOW WAS MERCURY DISCOVERED?

We have known about it since the ancient time and it was utilized by civilizations including Ancient China and Ancient Egypt.

The first Emperor of China, Qin Shi Huang, thought that it would make him live forever since it was considered part of the Elixir of Life. Unfortunately, since mercury is toxic, consuming it probably killed him.

Alchemists, for several years, believed that it was the "prima materia" and the other metals could all be made from it. They even though they could make gold from it.

Planet Mercury

WHERE DID ITS NAME COME FROM?

The name was derived from the planet Mercury which had been named for the swift messenger of the Roman gods, whose name was Mercury. Since it flows quickly when in its liquid form, it was given the name of Mercury. Its symbol, Hg, is derived from "hydragyrum", which is the Latin term for "liquid silver".

ISOTOPES

Mercury contains seven stable isotopes. Mercury-202 which is comprised of about 30% of all mercury, is the most plentiful in nature.

ELEMENTS

A pure substance created from a single type of atom is known as an element. The element is the building block for the rest of the matter of the world. Helium, gold, hydrogen, oxygen, and iron are all considered elements.

The atomic number is important to an element. This represents how many protons are in an atom. Every element's atomic number is unique. The first element is Hydrogen

Hydrogen
H_2

which contains one proton, therefore its atomic number is 1. Gold contains 79 protons in every atom and its atomic number is 79.

8.151
14 Si
2.33
1410
Silicium
72.64

In their standard state, elements contain a certain number of protons and electrons. Silicon, which has the atomic number of 14, is important for electronics.

Even though they are made from the same types of atoms, they can still be in diverse forms. Dependent upon the temperature, they can be a solid, gas, or liquid.

Also, they can become different forms depending how tight the atoms are packed. These are known by allotropes. An example is carbon. Depending on how its atoms fit, they can form graphite, coal, or diamond.

Currently, there are 118 elements. Only 94 of these are believed to exist on Earth naturally.

Graphite

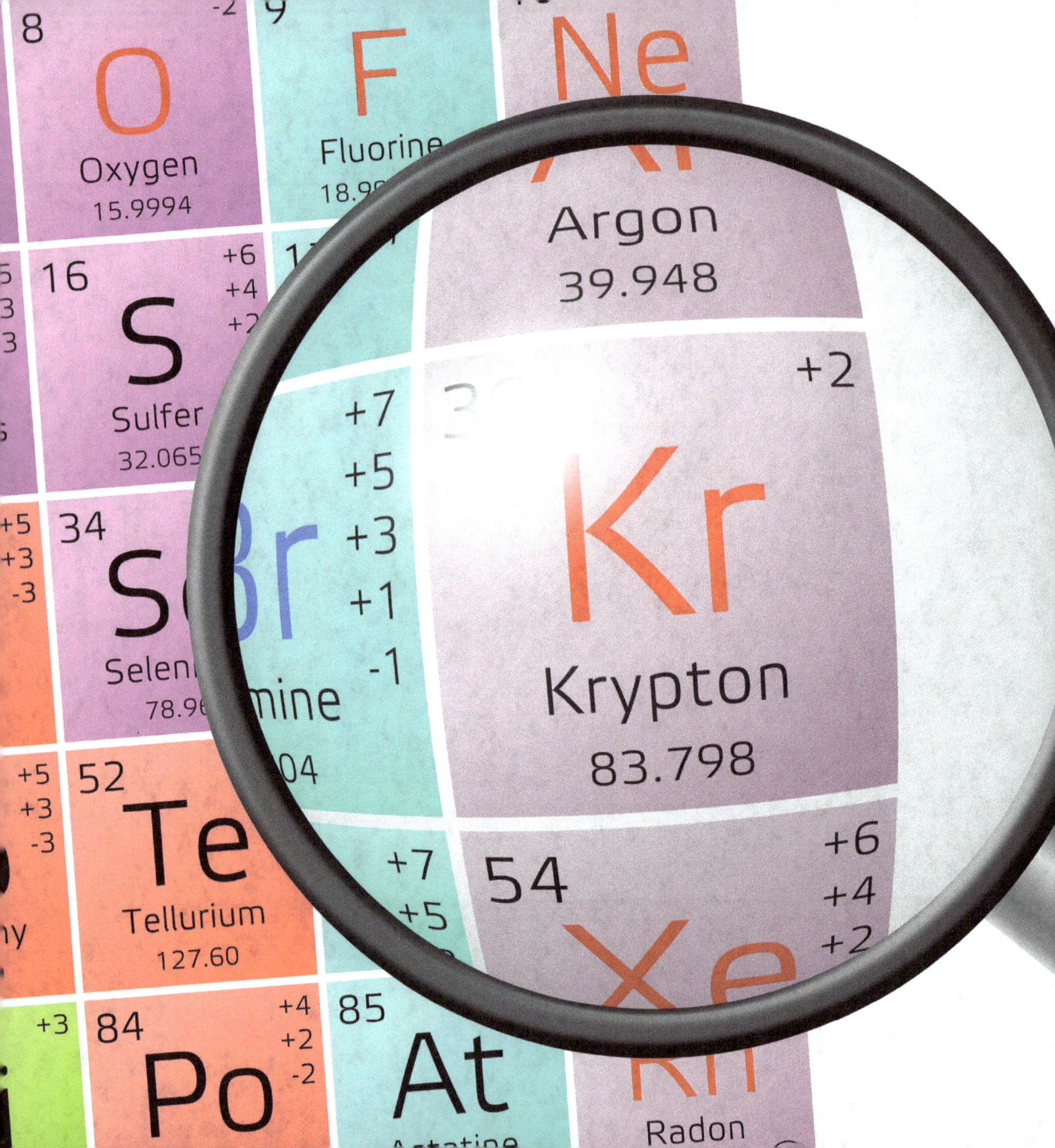

O
Oxygen
15.9994
F
Fluorine
18.99
Ne
Argon
39.948
16
S
Sulfer
32.065
+6
+4
+2
+2
Kr
Krypton
83.798
34
Se
Seleni
78.96
Br
mine
+7
+5
+3
+1
-1
52
Te
Tellurium
127.60
+5
+3
-3
54
Xe
+7
+5
+6
+4
+2
84
Po
+4
+2
-2
+3
85
At
Astatine
Rn
Radon

Sometimes elements are grouped together if they contain similar properties. Some are listed here:

Noble Gases – Xenon, radon, krypton, argon, neon, and helium are noble gases. The outer shell of their atoms are full of electrons. Because of this, they do not react much with the other elements. They are used a lot in signs since they produce a glow of vibrant colors as an electrical current passes through them.

Alkali Metals – Potassium, sodium, and lithium are examples of alkali metals. They contain only 1 electron in their outer shell and are quite reactive.

Other groups include lanthanides, actinides, alkali earth metals, transition metals, nonmetals, and halogens.

Lithium Ion Battery
Li-ion BATTERY

ISOTOPES OF OXYGEN

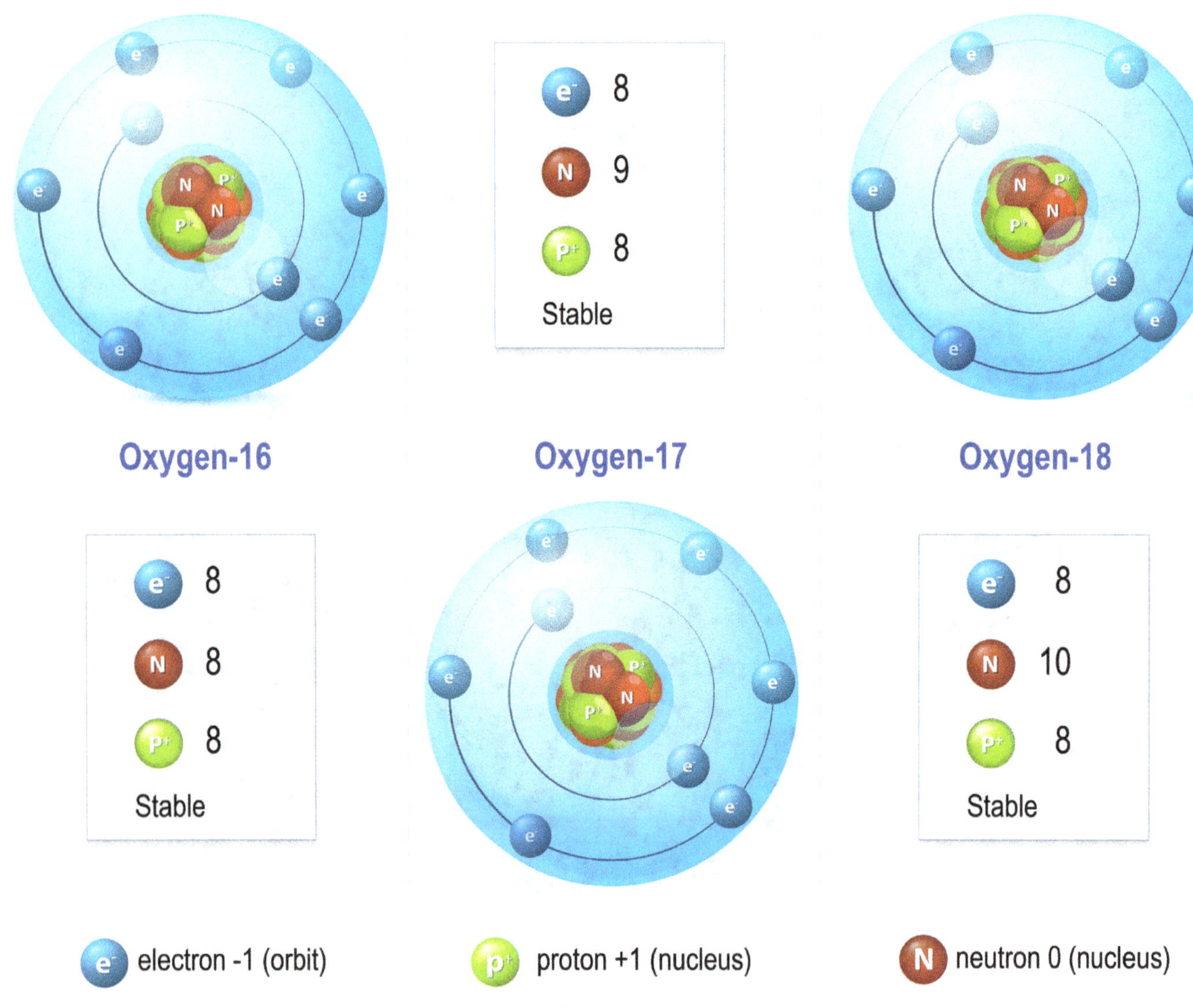

ISOTOPES

Atoms that contain identical numbers of electrons and protons, but contain different numbers of neutrons are called Isotopes. If the number of neutrons is changed, the element remains the same. Atoms with differing neutron numbers are referred to as "isotopes" of the element.

Because the neutron does not have an electrical charge, altering the number of the neutrons does not affect the element's chemistry. However, it will alter its mass. Isotopes are recognized by their mass, being the total number of neutrons and protons.

ISOTOPES OF CARBON

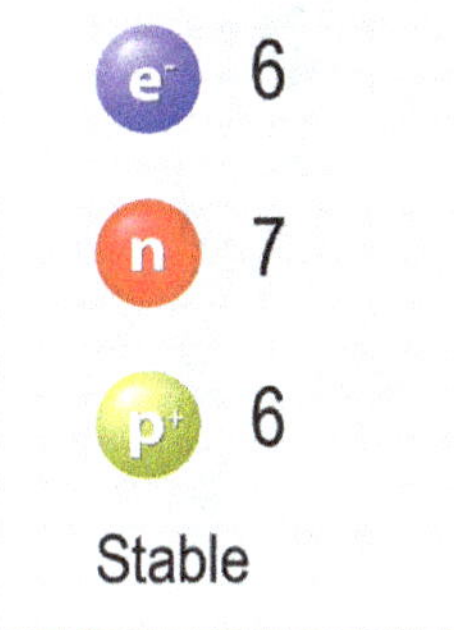
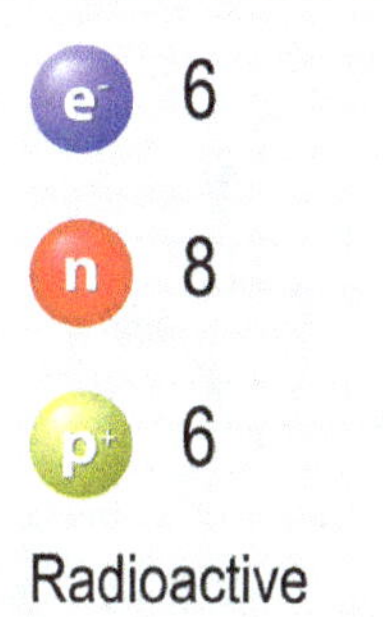

Carbon-12

e⁻	6
n	6
p⁺	6

Stable

Carbon-13

e⁻	6
n	7
p⁺	6

Stable

Carbon-14

e⁻	6
n	8
p⁺	6

Radioactive

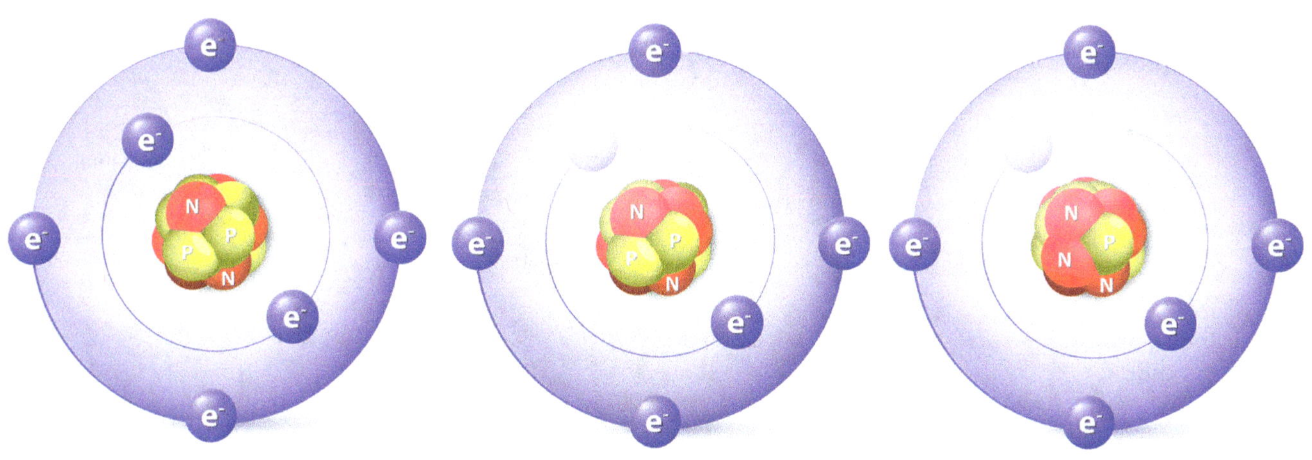

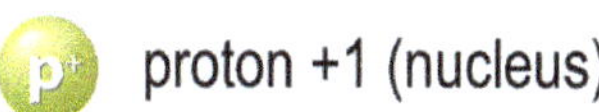

ISOTOPES OF NITROGEN

Nitrogen-14

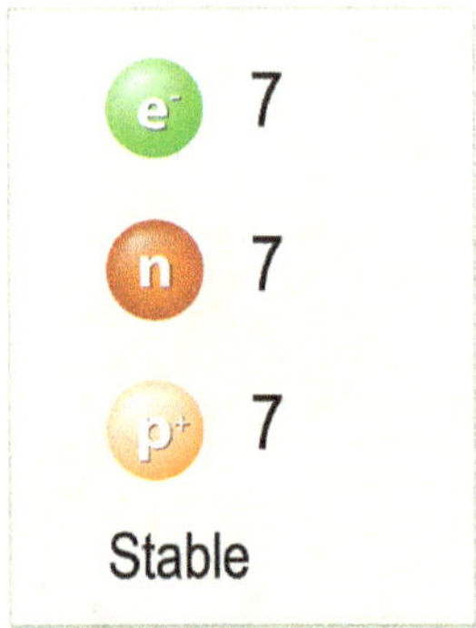

Nitrogen-15

Nitrogen-16

Isotopes are typically written in two ways. They will both utilize the atom's mass, where mass = (number of protons) + (number of neutrons). The first method is to indicate the mass in superscript in front of the symbol of the element:

- ^{235}U.

- ^{14}C

- ^{4}He

The second method is writing it out; placing the mass following a dash next to the element's name:

- uranium-238

- carbon-14

- helium-4

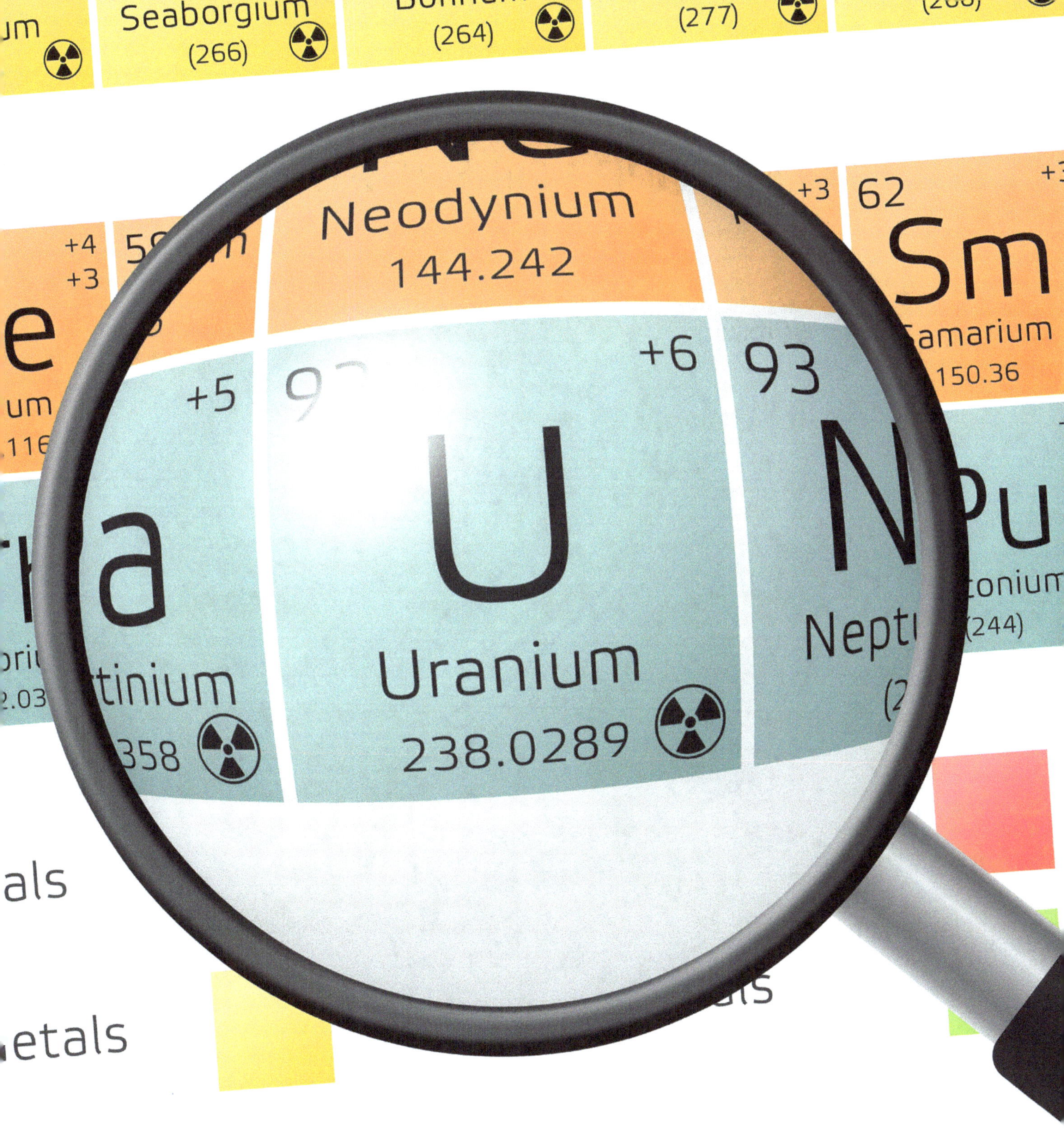

Seaborgium
(266)
Bohrium
(264)
(277)
(266)
Neodynium
144.242
62
Sm
Samarium
150.36
+4
+3
59
+3
+6
93
+5
92
U
Uranium
238.0289
N
Np
Neptu
conium
(244)
+3
116
a
tinium
358
Pu
als
etals

ISOTOPES OF HYDROGEN

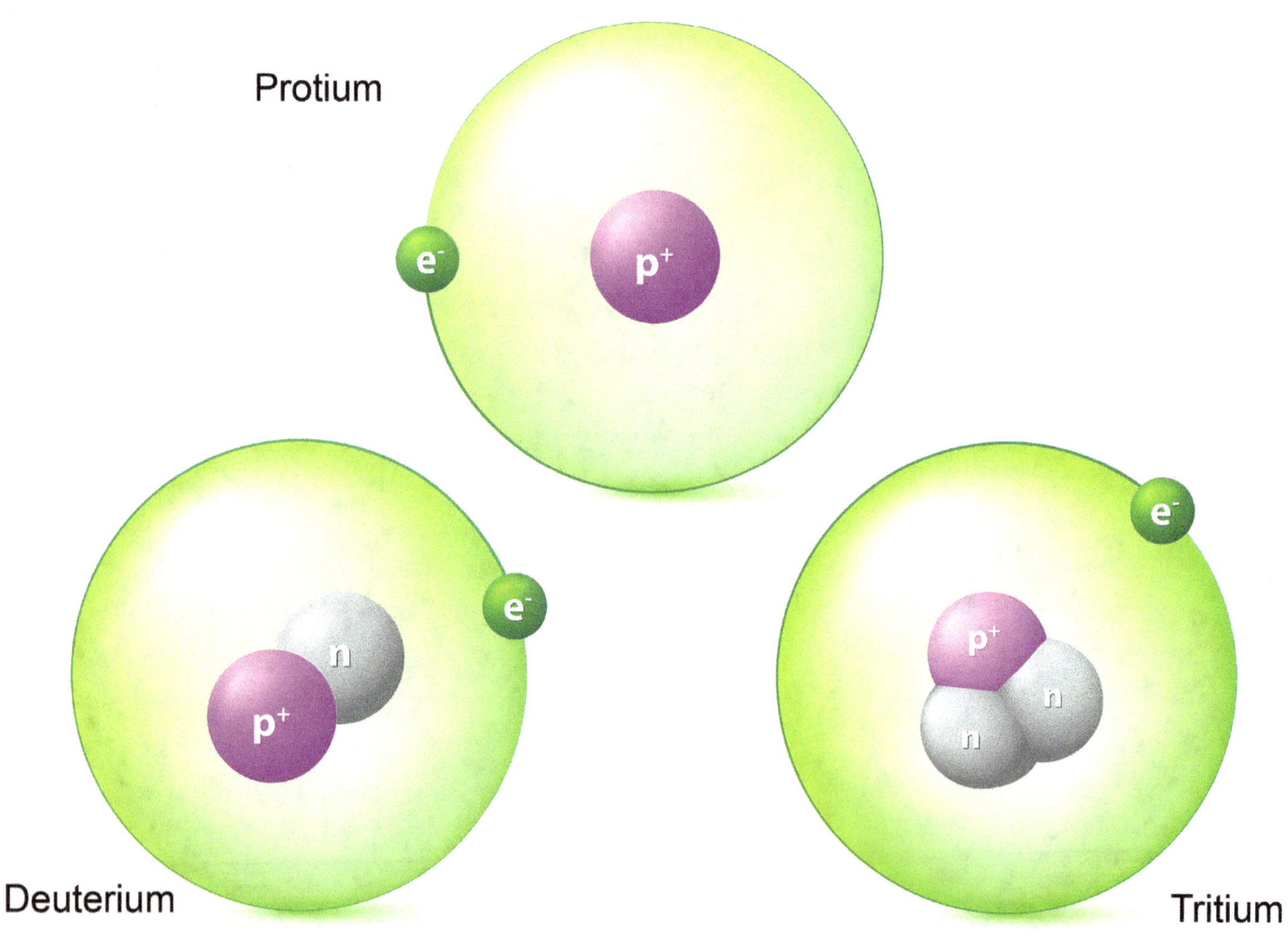

The only element that has isotopes with specific names is hydrogen. In its common form, containing zero neutrons, it is known as protium. If it has one neutron it is called deuterium and with two neutrons it is known as tritium.

All elements contain a certain number of isotopes. With only three isotopes, hydrogen has the lowest number of isotopes.

Isotopes can be either stable or unstable. An unstable isotope will decay in time and eventually become a different element or isotope. An unstable isotope is believed to be radioactive. Most of the elements which can be found in nature consist of stable isotopes. Tin is considered to be the most stable isotope, consisting of ten various stable isotopes.

50
2
8
18
18
4
Sn
Tin
118.71

PERIODIC TABLE OF THE ELEMENTS

Long Shadow Style

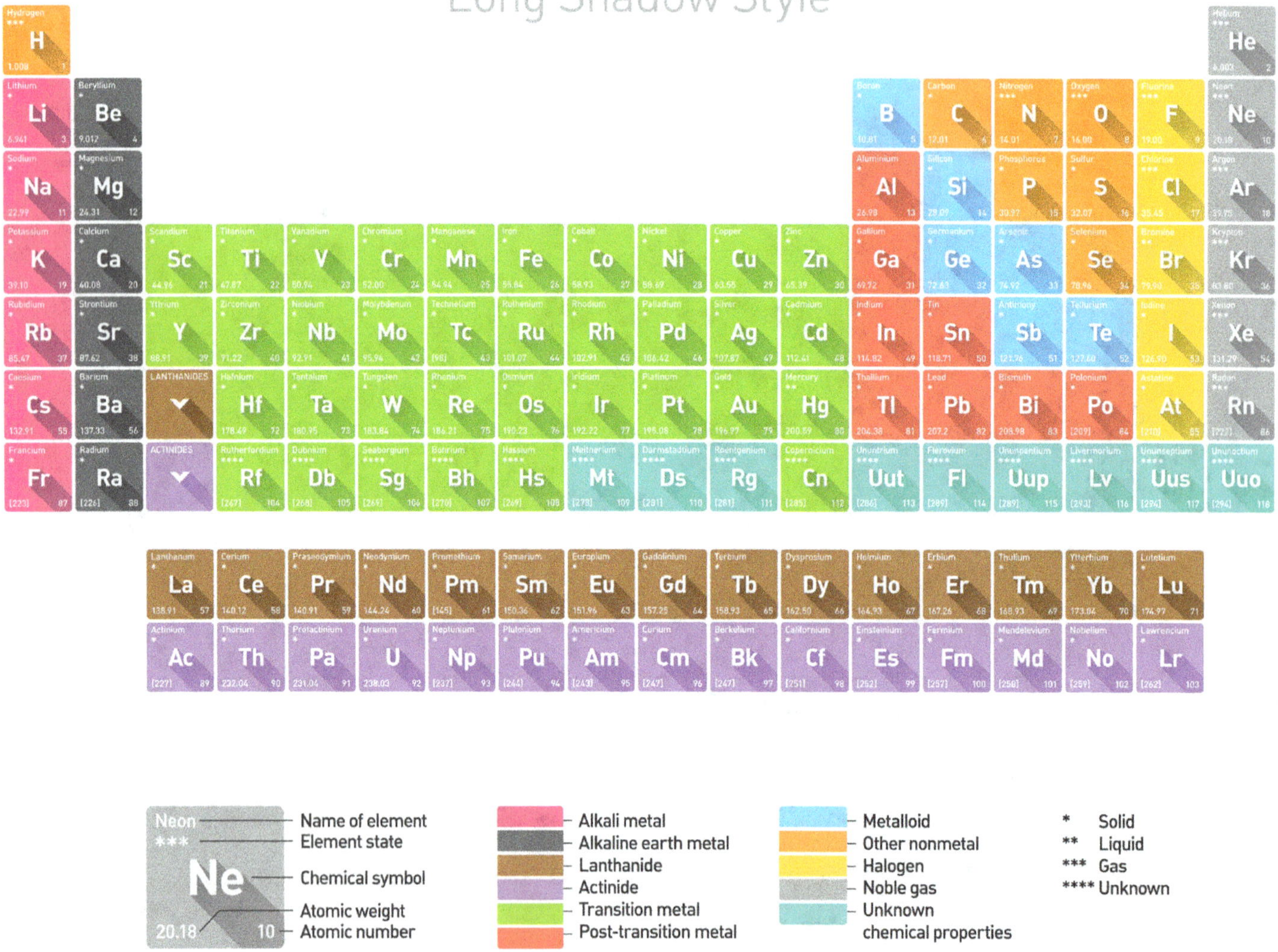

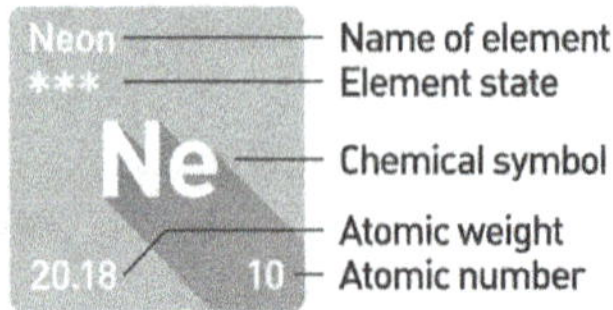

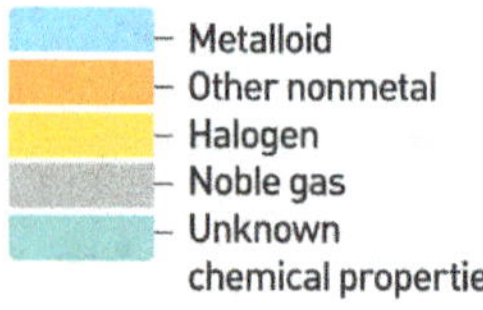

THE PERIODIC TABLE OF ELEMENTS

The Periodic Table of Elements is how the elements are listed. The elements are categorized by their atom's structure, including their number of protons, and the number of electrons contained in its outer shell. The elements are listed from top to bottom and left to right in order by their atomic number, the atom's number of protons.

It is named "periodic" because the elements are lined up in periods of cycles. The elements are lined up from left to right in rows based on the number of protons contains in their nucleus (atomic number). Some of the columns have been skipped so that elements containing identical number of valence electrons are able to line up in the same column.

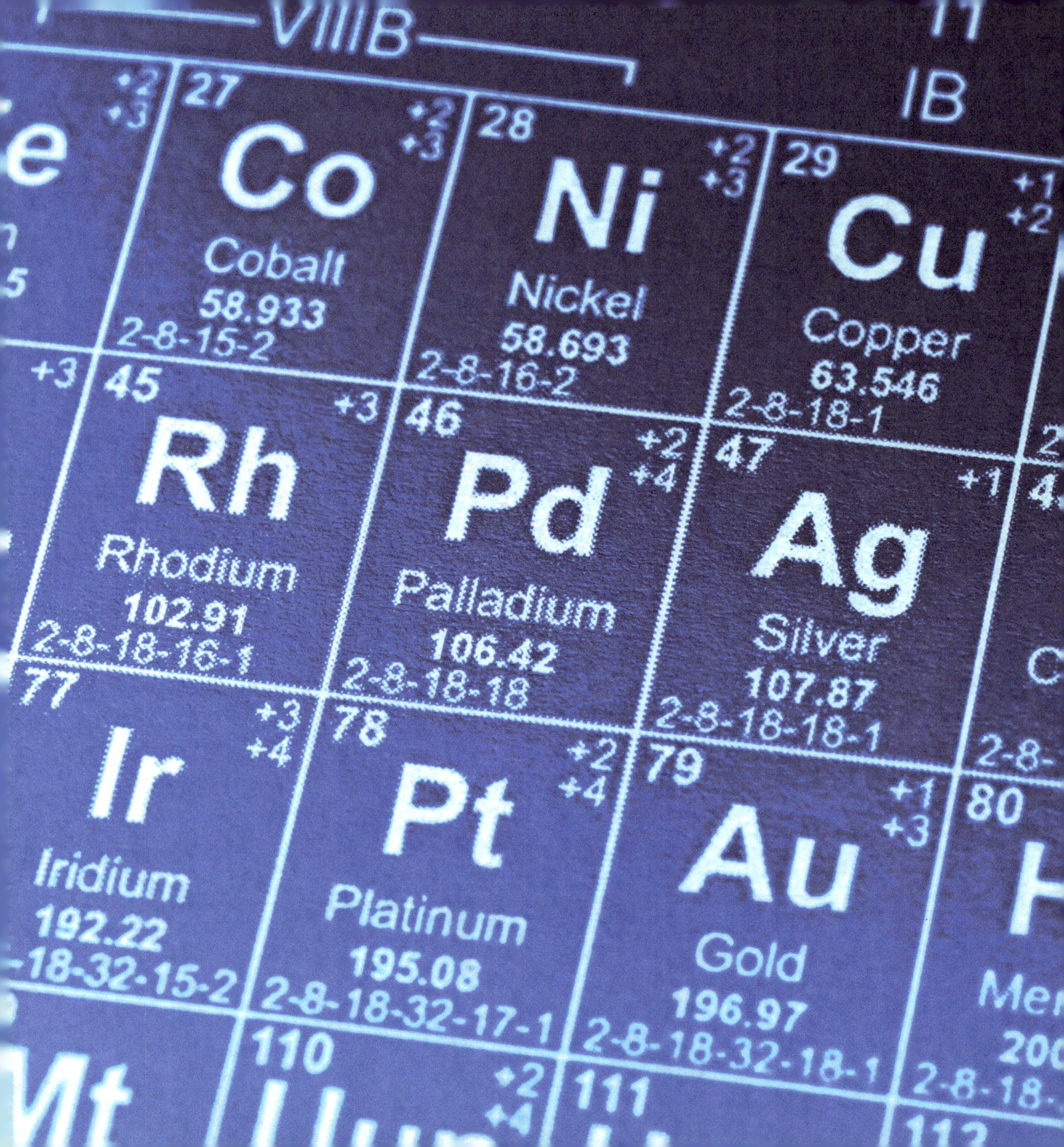

VIIIB

IB

+2
+3
27
Co
Cobalt
58.933
2-8-15-2

+2
+3
28
Ni
Nickel
58.693
2-8-16-2

+2
+3
29
Cu
Copper
63.546
2-8-18-1

+3
45
Rh
Rhodium
102.91
2-8-18-16-1

+3
46
Pd
Palladium
106.42
2-8-18-18

+2
+4

47
Ag
Silver
107.87
2-8-18-18-1

+1

77
Ir
Iridium
192.22
-18-32-15-2

+3
+4
78
Pt
Platinum
195.08
2-8-18-32-17-1

+2
+4

79
Au
Gold
196.97
2-8-18-32-18-1

+1
+3

80
2-8-

110
Uun

+2
+4

111
Uuu

112
200
2-8-18-

Mt

E ach horizontal row is known as a period. There are seven, possibly eight, periods total. The first period has only two elements and is short, helium and hydrogen. The sixth one contains 32 elements. The element to the far left of each period contains 1 electron in its outer shell, while the ones to the far right contain a full shell.

Now that you have learned about Mercury, you might want to find a thermometer and figure out where the mercury is and what it does.

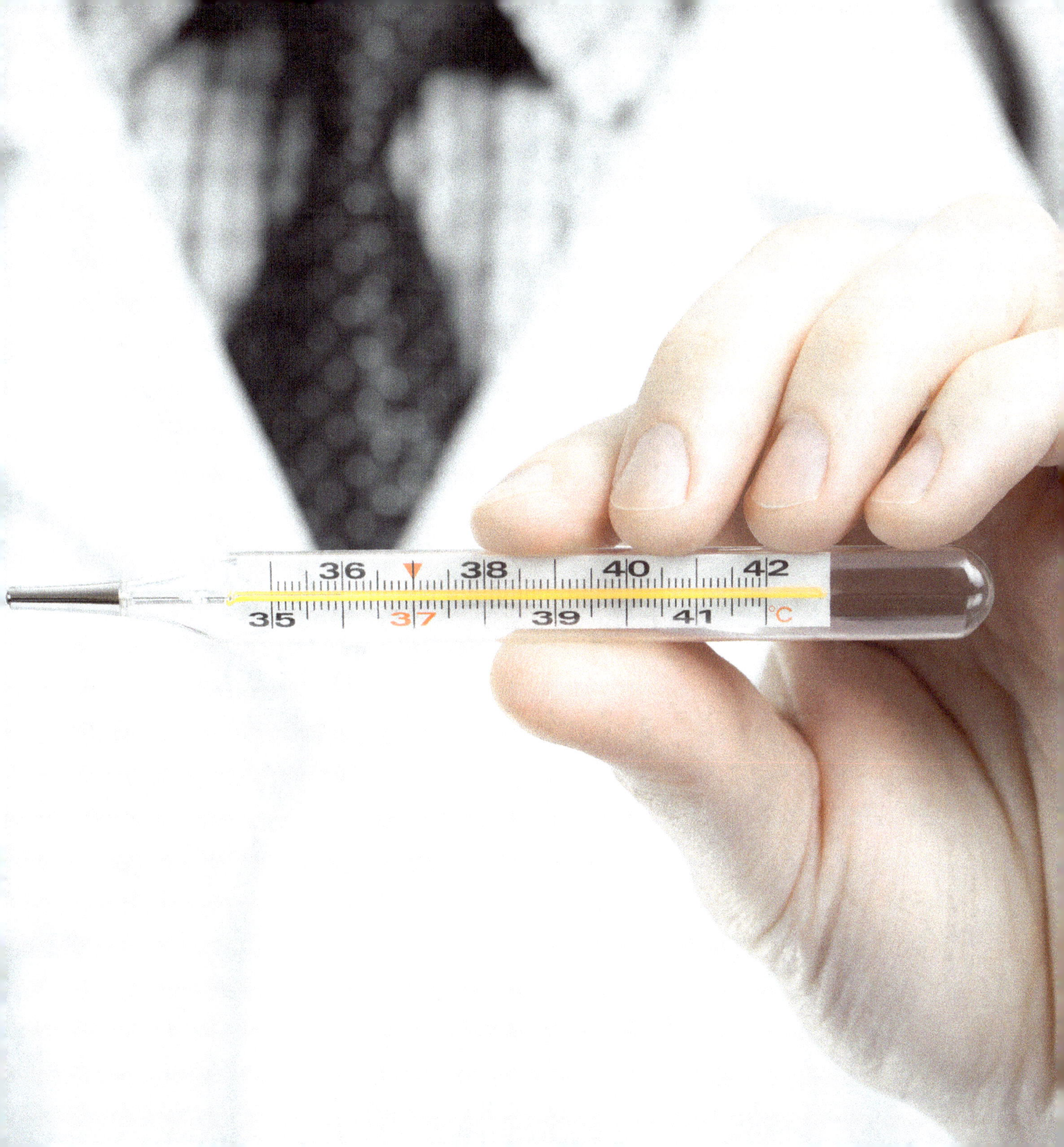

35
36
37
38
39
40
41
42
°C

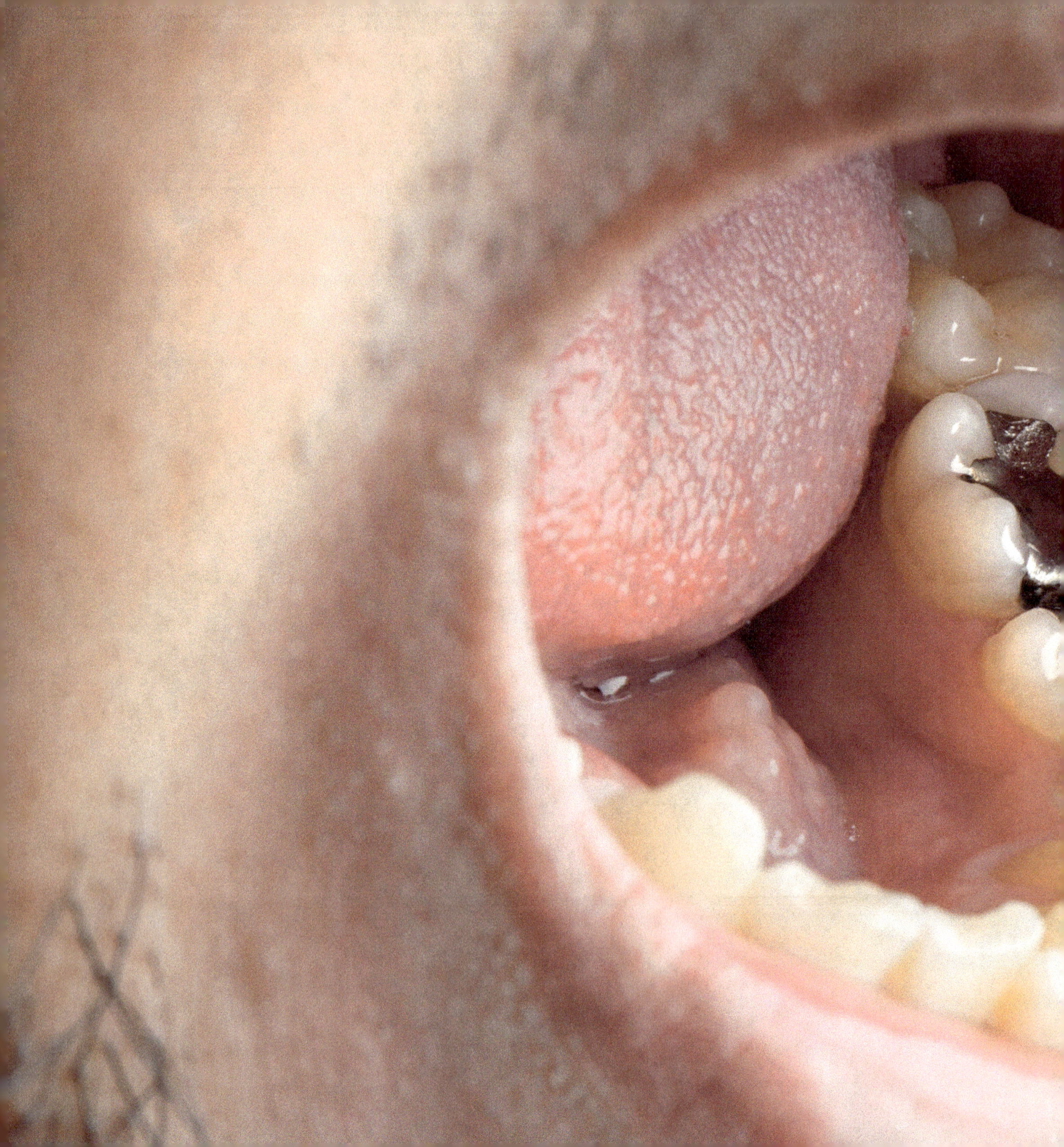

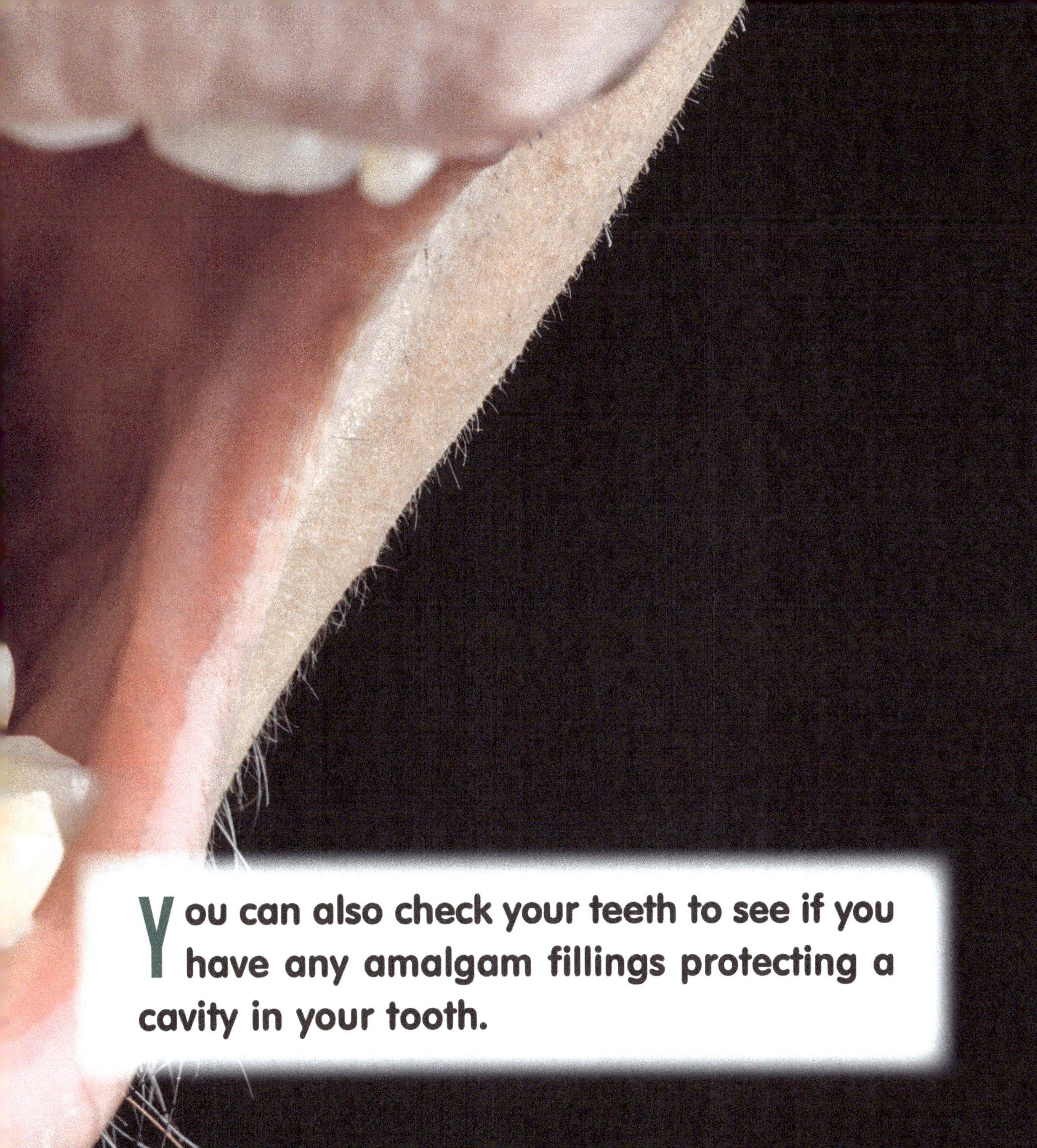

You can also check your teeth to see if you have any amalgam fillings protecting a cavity in your tooth.

For additional information, you can go to your
local library, research the internet, and ask
questions of your teachers, family, and friends.

Visit
BABY PROFESSOR
EDUCATION KIDS
www.BabyProfessorBooks.com
to download Free Baby Professor eBooks and view
our catalog of new and exciting Children's Books

www.ingramcontent.com/pod-product-compliance
Lightning Source LLC
Chambersburg PA
CBHW060130120726
48003CB00009B/2842